Ask the
RIGHT
Questions

Get the Right
ANSWERS
for Sound Financial
Retirement Planning

ROBB HILL

ISBN: 978-0-9985900-0-4

Published in the United States of America

Ask the **RIGHT** Questions
Get the Right **ANSWERS**
for Sound Financial Retirement Planning

Robb Hill's *Ask the Right Questions, Get the Right Answers* is a concise and straight forward guide to securing your financial future. Over the past century individual financial security after retirement has taken many dips and dives and has gone through an immense amount of changes. Mr. Hill addresses past retirement practices starting with the first corporate pensions. He takes us through some history as to why these pensions were created and how they are being dismantled, the roll Congress plays in protecting corporations while individual's promised pensions are collapsing like a house of cards, and then explains the shift to funds like 401Ks.

Mr. Hill's book explores the financial options available in preparing for retirement and some situations why other options may be better then others for some people. He feeds us just enough information to give us an understanding but is not overwhelming. He guides us through choosing a financial advisor and gives us the questions to ask. He explains how financial advisors make their money and when to steer clear or be wary. Surprisingly there are only four main areas that are essential to have in place and I felt empowered knowing that at my age I have a few of them in place and a few I need to explore and secure. The task is not as daunting as I've thought.

Robb Hill includes a lot of statistics and backs up his facts. The excerpt that really stood out to me in this guide was this: "Take 100 people at the beginning of their working career's...40 years later, according to the Social Security Administration, one will be wealthy, five will be financially secure, five will continue working, 36 will be dead and 54 will be dependent upon their meager Social Security checks, relatives, friends or even charity for a minimum standard of living. Planning is the major difference between the 6% that were successful and the 94% that failed to accomplish their objectives."

Ask the Right Questions, Get the Right Answers is 110 pages of rich content that everyone should read, even if you feel you have your bases covered, regardless of your age, to gain an understanding of what you should have in place in order to be comfortable during your retirement years. This is phenomenal guide to read to gain knowledge and raise questions with your own financial advisor. For those who don't have professional help, it gives you an understanding of what you should have in place, even if you do it yourself. Ask the Right Questions, Get the Right Answers is available in eBook format and in paperback.

Jackie Miller, Co-Founder of **AuthorsDen.com**

Contents

Part 4:

Dedication

This book is dedicated to my wife, Ruth, for her tireless belief and for her love that I have been privileged to experience, our children Abraham and Elizabeth, for being wonderful, outstanding children.

Last but not least, to my mother, Hattie J Hill, may she rest in peace.

Acknowledgments

First, I wish to thank God for everything!

For all your help around the house, thank you, Aunt Martha. For Pops and my step-mother, Nora, and my brothers and sisters, thank you for believing in me.

With special thanks to Great Life Educational Academy, Brokers' Choice of Colorado, Dave Wang of AIL, and a host of others.

All names and locations used in the examples in this book have been changed to ensure privacy. The examples are true financial situations encountered by R Hill Enterprises, Inc.

Poor Is a State of Mind

The goal of this book is to impart to you, the reader, a basic understanding of financial planning considerations and why they are necessary. I pray that the information contained in these pages will assist you in formulating a financial plan that will cover all the bases, fill in the gaps, and ensure that you will avoid the many problems that can arise as you reach your golden years.

As I write this book, I have been in the financial services industry now for fifteen years. It has been my observation over the years that many of the people that I've counseled had no idea why they purchased this or that financial product. Most of the time, they bought something because the salesman said so, and they had no idea about all the different aspects of financial planning.

One of the first organizations that I worked for used an approach that I call the bait and switch. You are asked to respond to a free, no-obligation benefit you receive via mail in a flyer. The job for the insurance agent was to basically sell you a product that you had not requested. The home office and up-line management justified this practice by stating that everyone needs insurance.

Although the company was very profitable using this practice, I didn't like the idea of talking someone into something that they unknowingly requested. Needless to say, I didn't stay with that company very long. While I did make some money there, it was not my idea of being of service.

I then moved to another organization that I thought was the ultimate in insurance sales. The people that I was fortunate enough to call on had requested insurance. This was a no-brainer; all I had to do was just take their order. So I had been doing this for a while and then it dawned on me: I was only halfway helping these people who had returned the inquiry letter. So, I began to look more into other aspects of financial services.

I realized that to truly be of service, there was an education gap that I needed to bridge—I had to educate my clients about financial products and how to incorporate them into their financial plans. The biggest hurdle that I have encountered in this process and by far the hardest to overcome is to explain to people something that they think they already know about but really don't.

The concept of being poor is a state of mind that needs to be overcome; you need to realize that you do have a say in your financial well-being. The thought of being poor keeps many people stuck in poverty. The funny thing is that most people who consider themselves poor just have their priorities out of order, and a simple shift in thinking can make all the difference in their financial lives.

The goal of my company, R Hill
Enterprises, Incorporated, is to educate consumers. The formula for accomplishing this is through lectures in four areas of financial preparation: the first is on "Wills and Trusts"; the second is on "Long-Term Care"; the third is on "Safe Alternatives to the Stock Market"; and the fourth is on "Final Expenses." (See part 4: "Solution Mode.")

This book is about *education*; well, actually, a more precise term might be *training*. The reason why I changed terms is because education to me is being able to bring out of you a greater expression of what you already know. With these lectures, this *training*, I hope to impart some knowledge that you don't already know. So, for the sake of that definition, let's embark on the *training* that I have put together.

Part 1
The Wake-Up Call

Chapter 1

It's a Consumer-Driven Economy

As I was growing up and learning from my elders, it became clear that you work to get what you want. As I have gotten older and more informed, I learned that this mentality of "working to get what you want" is only half of the truth.

We must revisit the past in order to gain some insight into our current situation: In short, the Depression of the '30s began early for farmers and the working class. In 1929, just before the bust, when poverty-level income was estimated at $1,000 per year, and a family of five needed $1,800 per year for "minimal health and decency," no less than 42 percent of all US families earned less than $1,500. Some workers, of course, were making it, particularly workers among those immigrant groups that included many artisans, tradespeople, and *skilled workers* (i.e., people who were already at the top of the working class, such as Jews). But for those less fortunate—Italians, French, Canadians, Poles, Ukrainians, and especially black Americans and Mexicans—the '20s provided no escape.

Nevertheless, prosperity and the rise of a consumer society did have a major impact on the middle class and on at least part of the working class, and it requires closer discussion.

Recall that as early as the 1890s, the American economy had shown signs of stagnation because of the apparent saturation of consumer markets. There were two readily apparent ways of solving this problem: (1) expansion of both trade and investment abroad, and (2) consumption at home. We will not discuss the former, for it only had an indirect impact on domestic social policy. As for the latter, to state the solution merely raises another problem: How could the consumption of the American people expand, given that most Americans were already spending every cent they earned to ensure bare survival?

The answer, in essence, was to persuade people to save less of their income (if they had any to save); to spend it all; and then go into debt—that is, to spend more than their income. "The future of business," wrote one trade magazine "lies in its ability to manufacture customers as well as products." [1]

Advertisements and the mass media were used to create the image of a consumer society, and in propagating the ideas of "right living," they did their part. [2]

What was needed, it should be emphasized, was nothing less than a major change in American values. "Industry," recalled Boston merchant Edward Filene some years later "was perfected to a point which made it absolutely necessary for the masses to spend their money freely and to unlearn their previous habits of thrift." Buy instead of save; consume instead of work; go into debt; live for today, not for tomorrow.

It is difficult to overstate the magnitude of the change in values the new consumer society required and created, but this mentality had a much greater price: many working-class people became dependent in their later years.

My childhood was turbulent to put it mildly; I am from a broken family and I was raised by my mother with a younger sister and brother. There were times that were tough to say the least. We were on public aid, and I was ashamed of that. I used to be so embarrassed to go to the store with food stamps.

I made up my mind to learn what the difference was between the "haves" and the "have nots." In my quest, I have found that there are actually three groups: the "haves," the "have nots," and the "haven't paid for what they have." Being in the financial services arena has opened my eyes a great deal!

The term, "consumer-driven economy," has taken on new meaning to me as well as what it means to the people who are targeted by advertising on a continuous basis to spend, spend, and then spend some more. The consumer-driven economy is a reality that is wreaking havoc on the baby boomer generation.

At this point in my life, I have come to the conclusion that we each have two options: "manage" debt or "create" wealth. The key word is "create."

The vast majority of the people that I come in contact with on a professional level are stuck in the management of debt, and odds are, if you have payments now, you will until you die.

However, there is a way out, and I hope the following chapters and my training will show you that way.

Chapter 2

Why this Idea Won't Work

In today's fast-paced, global economy, the majority of people are coming face-to-face with the fact that they will not be able to retire the way they would like to. Most people think that "retirement" is an age; I submit to you that retirement has nothing to do with age and everything to do with a person's financial position!

In our school system, "academic intelligence" is very important, and this is what our educational system teaches. In essence, what our school system teaches is how to be an *employee* [3] — very strange in the land of opportunity! The indoctrination starts at a very young age, it is very subtle, and begins when you are asked questions like, "What do you want to be when you grow up?

There are many forms of intelligence; for instance, there is "financial intelligence," but for there to be financial intelligence, there first has to be "financial literacy." [4] The question I have been asking of many people between the ages of fifty and seventy is: "What would you do differently if you were my age, and know what you know now?" The answer is always, "Get more education so that I could have gotten a better job to make more money!"

The next question is: "Have you come to grips emotionally that many older Americans will be destitute in ten to fifteen years?" This is according to Dr. Gary North who cites these interesting facts:

- Between 1995 and 2005, the number of workers who were age 55 and older increased by roughly 31% from 16,000,000 to 21,000,000.

- More than 33,000,000 people are age 65 or older in the United States today. By the year 2030, this population is likely to exceed 70,000,000, i.e., more than double.

- At age 65, 45% of Americans depend on relatives for financial support, 30% depend on charities, and 23% keep on working. Only 2% are self-supporting.
- Of all Americans who are 50 years old, 75% have less than $5,000 in the bank for retirement. [5]

The prevailing thought in my mind is, "If college is supposed to prepare you for life, what explains its failure to teach the very basics of success: How to build enough assets to achieve, eventually, both freedom and security?"[6] If the people in our teaching institutions ever learn this very important lesson, they will have to realize that a new teacher is necessary, one that has achieved both freedom and security. In retirement, the goal is not to have a pile of assets; the goal is cash flow.[7] The terms "laid-off," "downsized," "right-sized," and "Enroned" are very common today. A lot of people are realizing that "job security" is an oxymoron. There are thousands of college grads who are underemployed or unemployed because they are too expensive to hire.

"Security vs. freedom, in 1773, the year of the infamous Boston Tea Party, what were the American rebels protesting?" asked Rich Dad.

"Taxes," I replied. "We wanted freedom from taxes. Those brave men risked jail or prison by performing a criminal act against Mother England."

"Good," said Rich Dad. "So they did not throw the tea overboard in the name of greater job security?"

"No, they were willing to fight for freedom, not job security," I answered.

"And what do we teach in school today?" asked Rich Dad. "What is the main reason parents and teachers fearfully insist their kids study hard and get good grades? Is it for freedom?"

"No," I said quietly. "Parents and teachers want their kids to get good grades for job security... hopefully to get a high-paying job."[8] Most Americans are following a plan that will not work. This forty-year plan came about because of the Industrial Revolution. Manufacturing needed a lot of workers. Where were they going to get these workers from? At that time, the answer to that question was from all the farmers and small business owners.

The owners of industry realized that in order to get these people to leave their farms and their small businesses, there had to be an incentive! This is where the promise of "after working thirty years, the company will take care of you in your old age" came from. This promise brought thousands of people out of the fields and into the factories. With the advent of WW I and WW II, the United States of America emerged as the world's supreme manufacturing superpower.

Now fast forward; we find ourselves in the age of political correctness with the first ever business-minded American president of the great United States of America, President elect Donald J Trump and the subject of a lot of scrutiny.

In my opinion, the state of the United States of America can be tied directly to career politicians who have no idea about business matters; and we have the largest segment of the population, known as the baby boomers, moving at an amazing clip toward this place called retirement, and we now find ourselves faced with too much government, too many taxes, not enough jobs, and an unheard of deficit; all this is now in the hands of our new president Donald Trump.

The solutions to these problems are another book altogether, so I will not address them here; as for our personal economies, the solution to that problem *is* in our hands.

The problem that I want to address in the remainder of this book is the lack of consumer education in the area of financial planning. And here is where we start.

Part 2
The Problem

Chapter 3

The Great Retirement Rip-Off

According to an issue of *Time Magazine* dated October 31, 2005 (the cover story was entitled "The Great Retirement Rip-off"), "Millions of Americans who think they will retire with benefits are in for a nasty surprise. How corporations are picking people's pockets—with the help of Congress!"[9]

The Broken Promise

It was part of the American dream, a pledge made by corporations to their workers: For your decades of turmoil, you'll be assured of retirement benefits like a pension and health care. Now more and more companies are walking away from those promises, leaving millions of Americans at risk of an impoverished retirement. How can this be legal? This *Time* investigation story looked at how Congress let it happen and the widespread "social insecurity" it was causing.

The little shed behind Joy Whitehouse's modest home is filled with aluminum cans—soda cans, soup cans, and vegetable cans—that she collects from neighbors or finds during her periodic expeditions along the roadside. Two times a month, she takes them to a recycler who pays her as much as $30 for her harvest of castoffs. When your fixed income is $942 a month, an extra $30 here and there makes a big difference. After paying rent, utilities, and car and life insurance, Whitehouse is left with less than $40 a week to cover everything else. So the money from cans helps pay medical bills for the cancer and chronic lung disease she has been battling for years as well as food expenses. "I eat a lot of soup," says the tiny, spirited sixty-nine-year-old, who lives in Majestic Meadows, a mobile-home park for senior citizens near Salt Lake City, Utah.

Whitehouse never envisioned spending her later years this way. She and her husband, Alva Don, raised four children. In the 1980s, they lived in Montana where he earned a good living as a long-haul truck driver for Pacific Intermountain Express. But in 1986, he was killed on the job in a highway accident attributed to faulty maintenance on his truck as his company struggled to survive the cutthroat pricing of congressionally ordered deregulation. After her husband's death, Whitehouse knew the future would be tough, but she was confident in her economic survival. After all, the company had promised her a death benefit of $598 every two weeks for the rest of her life—a commitment she had in writing, one that was a matter of law.

She received the benefit payments until October 1990, when the check bounced. A corporate-takeover artist later sent to prison for ripping off a pension fund and other financial improprieties, had stripped down the business and forced it into the US Bankruptcy Court. There, the obligation was erased, thanks to congressional legislation that gives employers the right to walk away from agreements with their employees.

To support herself, Whitehouse had already sold the couple's Montana home and moved to the Salt Lake City area where she had family and friends. With her savings running out, she applied early (at a reduced rate) for her husband's Social Security. She needed every penny. For health reasons, she couldn't work. She had undergone a double mastectomy. An earlier cancer of the uterus had eaten away at her stomach muscles so that a metal plate and artificial bladder were installed. Her children and other relatives offered to help, but Whitehouse is fiercely self-sufficient. Friends and neighbors pitch in to fill her shed with aluminum.

"You put your pride in your pocket, and you learn to help yourself," she says. "I save cans."

Through no fault of her own, Whitehouse had found herself thrust into the ranks of workers and their spouses—previously invisible but now growing fast— who believed the corporate promises about retirement and health care often affirmed by the Federal Government: they would receive a guaranteed pension; they would have company-paid health insurance until they qualified for Medicare; they would receive company-paid supplemental medical insurance after turning sixty-five; they would receive a fixed-death benefit in the event of a fatal accident that befell their spouse; and they would have a modest life insurance policy.

They didn't get those things. And they won't. Corporate promises are often not worth the paper they're printed on. Businesses in one industry after another are revoking long-standing commitments to their workers. It's the equivalent of your bank telling you that it needs the money you put into your savings account more than you do—and then keeping it.

The result is a wholesale downsizing of the American Dream. It began in the 1980s with the elimination of middle-class, entry-level jobs in lower-paying industries—apparel, textiles, and shoes, among others. More recently, it has spread to jobs that paid solid, middle-class wages, starting with the steel industry, then the airlines, and then autos—with no end in sight.

That's why Whitehouse, as difficult as her situation is, is worried more about how her children and grandchildren will cope. And well she should. Because while her story is the tale of millions of older Americans; it is also a window into the future for many millions more.

The *Time* investigation story previously cited has concluded that long before today's working Americans reach retirement age, policy decisions by Congress favoring corporate and special interests over workers will drive millions of older Americans—a majority of them women—into poverty, push millions more to the brink, and turn retirement years into a time of need for everyone but the affluent.

The transition is well under way, eroding efforts of the past three decades to eliminate poverty among the aging. From taxes to health care to pensions, Congress has enacted legislation that adds to the cost of retirement and eats away at dollars once earmarked for food and housing. These reversals of fortune are staggering, and even those already retired or near retirement will be squeezed by changing economic rules.

And let's make no bones about it; Congress's role has been

pivotal. Law-makers wrote bankruptcy regulations to allow corporations to scrap the health insurance they promised employees who retired early—sometimes voluntarily, quite often not. They wrote pension rules that encouraged corporations to underfund their retirement plans or switch to plans less favorable to employees. They denied workers the right to sue to enforce retirement promises. The introduction and implementation of the Affordable Care Act otherwise known as Obama care has created the world's most expensive medical care without any comparable benefit.

One by one, lawmakers have under-mined or destroyed policies that once afforded at least the possibility of a livable existence to many seniors, while at the same time encouraging corporations to repudiate lifetime-benefit agreements. All this under the guise of ensuring workers that they are in charge of their own destiny—such as it is.

The process accelerated dramatically during 2005. Two major US airlines, Delta and Northwest, turned to bankruptcy court to cut costs and delay pension fund contributions. This followed earlier bankruptcy filings by United Airlines and US Airways, both of which jettisoned their guaranteed pension plans. Then on October 8, 2005 the largest US auto parts maker, Delphi Corp., filed for bankruptcy protection, seeking to cut off medical and life insurance benefits for its retirees. Delphi's pension funds are short $11 billion.

According to Elizabeth Warren, a Harvard law professor and Democrat Senator from Massachusetts who specializes in bankruptcy, this is just going to get worse as ever more companies see the value to their bottom line of "scraping off" employee obligations. "There's no business in America that isn't going to figure out a way to get rid of these benefit promises"

That may include the world's largest automaker, General Motors. Although GM chairman Rick Wagoner has insisted that "we don't consider bankruptcy to be a viable business strategy," some on Wall Street are skeptical given the company's array of problems. Their view was reinforced when GM, the company that dominated the American economy through the twentieth century, announced on October 17, 2005 that it had reached a precedent-setting agreement with the United Auto Workers leadership to rescind $1 billion worth of health-care benefits for its retirees. If ratified by the union membership, the retrenchment will hasten the end to company-subsidized health care for all retirees.

From 1988 to 2015; the drop in the share of large employers (200+ workers) offering retiree health coverage went from 66 percent in 1988 to 23 percent in 2015.[10] The end result: a fresh and additional burden on retirees concluded a 2015 report by the Kaiser Family Foundation and Hewitt Associates."[11] For the majority of workers who retire before they turn age sixty-five and are eligible for Medicare, the coverage provided under employer plans is often difficult, if not impossible to find anywhere else."[12] For retirees over sixty-five, "Employer plans remain the primary source of prescription drug coverage for seniors on Medicare .... This coverage is more generous than the standard prescription drug benefit that will be offered by Medicare plans beginning in 2016.[13]

Perhaps the best yardstick to assess the outlook for the later years is the defined-benefit pension, long the gold standard for retirement because it guarantees a fixed income for life. The number of such plans offered by corporations has plunged from 112,200 in 1985 to 29,700 in 2005 and just 99, or about 20%, of Fortune 500 companies offered a defined benefit plan to new salaried employees in 2015, down from 104, or nearly 21% in 2014, and a dramatic fall from a decade earlier in 2005, when 248, or just over 48% of Fortune 500 firms, offered the plans. Since 1985, the number of active workers covered under defined benefit plans in the private sector declined from 22 million to 17 million 2005. They are the last members of what once promised to be the United States golden retirement era, and they are fast disappearing. From 2001 to 2004 nearly two hundred FORTUNE 1000 corporations killed or froze their defined-benefit plans. Today, 2016 just 24 Fortune 500 companies still offered traditional defined benefit plans to new salaried employees, a huge drop from the 138 companies that offered such plans in 2005.[14]

In 2005, Hewlett-Packard, long one of the most admired companies in the United States, pulled the plug on guaranteed pensions for new workers. An HP spokesman said the company had concluded that "pension plans are kind of a thing of the past." In that, HP was merely following the lead of business rival IBM and such other major companies as NCR Corp., Sears Holding Corp. and Motorola. The nation's largest employer, Wal-Mart, does not offer such pensions, either. At the current pace, human resources offices will turn out the lights in their defined-benefit section within a decade or so and this has become a reality for 2016 and at this point, individuals will assume all the risks for their retirement, just as they did one hundred years ago.

The shift away from guaranteed pensions was encouraged by Congress, which structured the rules in a way that invites corporations to abandon their defined-benefit plans in favor of defined-contribution plans, increasingly 401(k)s, in which employees set aside a fixed sum of money toward retirement. Many companies also contribute; some don't. Whatever the case, the contributions will never be enough to match the certain and long-term income from a defined-benefit plan.

What's more, once the money runs out, that's it. If people live longer than expected, get stuck with unanticipated expenses, or suffer losses of other once- promised benefits, they will have little besides their Social Security to sustain them.

This dawning perception among Americans that when it comes to retirement— "You're on your own, baby"—is surely a reason that President George Bush ran into so much opposition to his proposal to change Social Security from a risk-free plan into one with so-called private accounts. Critics of the seventy-year-old system were determined to chip away at Social Security as part of a larger effort to promote what the Bush Administration called an "ownership society."

Treasury Secretary John Snow told a congressional committee in February 2004: "I think we need to be concerned about pensions and the security that employees have in their pensions. And I think we need to encourage people to save and become part of an ownership society, which is very much a part of the president's vision for America." This was not the stance of the Obama administration which has pretty much encouraged the "nanny state" where government will take care of you.

Of course, it's much easier to own a piece of America when you have a pension like Snow's. When he stepped down as head of CSX Corporation—operator of the largest rail network in the Eastern United States—to take over the Treasury, Snow was given a lump-sum pension of $33.2 million. It was based on forty-four years of employment at CSX. Unlike most ordinary people who must work the actual years on which their pension is calculated, Snow was employed just twenty-six years. The additional eighteen years of his CSX employment history were fictional, a gift from the company's board of directors.

Snow is not alone. The "phantom employment record," as it might be called, is a common executive-retirement practice in corporate America—and one that is spelled-out in corporate filings with the Securities and Exchange Commission (SEC).

For example, Drew Lewis, the Pennsylvania Republican and onetime head of the US Department of Transportation, got a $1.5 million annual pension when he retired in 1996 as Chairman and CEO of Union Pacific Corp. His pension was based on thirty years of service to the company, but he actually worked there only eleven years. The other nineteen years of his employment history came courtesy of Union Pacific's board of directors, which included Vice President Dick Cheney.

And then there's Leo Mullin, the former Chairman and CEO of Delta Air Lines. Under Mullin's stewardship, Delta killed the defined-benefit pension of its nonunion workers and replaced it with a less generous plan. Now, a little more than a year after he retired the airline is in bankruptcy and can dump its pension obligations. But you need not fret about Mullin. On his way out the door, he picked up a $16 million retirement package. It's based on almost twenty-nine years of employment with Delta, at least twenty-one years more than he worked at the airline.

Chapter 4

How Your Savings Can Be Hijacked

At the same time corporate executives are paid retirement dollars for years they never worked, hapless employees lose supplemental retirement benefits for a lifetime of actual work.

Just ask Betty Moss. She was one of thousands of workers at Polaroid Corporation—the Waltham, Mass., maker of instant cameras and film—who, beginning in 1988, gave up 8 percent of their salary to underwrite an employee stock-ownership plan, or ESOP. It was created to thwart a corporate takeover and "to provide a retirement benefit" to Polaroid employees to supplement their pension, or so the company pledged.

Alas, it was not to be. Polaroid was slow to react to the digital revolution and began to lose money in the 1990s. From 1995 to 1998, the company racked up $359 million in losses. As its balance sheet deteriorated, so did the value of its stock, including shares in the ESOP. In October 2001, Polaroid sought bankruptcy protection from creditors.

By then, Polaroid's shares were virtually worthless, having plummeted from $60 in 1997 to less than the price of a Coke in October 2001. During that period, based on laws approved by Congress, employees were forbidden to unload their stock. But what employees weren't allowed to do at a higher price, the company-appointed trustee could do at the lowest possible price, without even seeking the workers' permission. Rather than wait for a possible return to profitability through restructuring, the trustee decided that it was "in the best interests" of the employees to sell the ESOP shares. They went for 9¢. In short order, a $300 million retirement nest egg put away by six thousand Polaroid employees was wiped out. Many lost between $100,000 and $200,000.

Betty Moss was one of the losers. Now sixty, she spent thirty-five years at Polaroid, beginning as a file clerk out of high school, and then working her way through college at night, and eventually rising to be senior regional operations manager in Atlanta.

"It was the kind of place people dream of working at," she said. "I can honestly say I never dreaded going to work. It was just the sort of place where good things were always happening."

One of those good things was supposed to be the ESOP touted by the company as a plan that "forced employees to save for their retirement," as Moss recalled. "Everybody went for it. We had been so conditioned to believe what we were told was true."

Once Polaroid entered bankruptcy, Moss and her retired co-workers learned a bitter lesson: They had no say in the security of benefits they had worked all their lives to accumulate. While the federal Pension Benefit Guaranty Corp. (PBGC) agreed to make good on most of their basic pensions, the rest of their benefits—notably the ESOP accounts, along with retirement, health care, and severance packages—were canceled.

The retirees, generally well educated and financially savvy, organized to try to win back some of what they had lost by petitioning bankruptcy court, which would decide how to divide the company's assets among creditors. To no avail; Polaroid's management had already undercut the employees' effort. Rather than file for bankruptcy in Boston, near the corporate offices, the company took its petition to Wilmington, Del., and a bankruptcy court that had developed a reputation for favoring corporate managers.

There, Polaroid's management contended that the company was in terrible financial shape and that the only option was to sell rather than reorganize. The retirees claimed that Polaroid executives were undervaluing the business so the company could ignore its obligations to retirees and sell out to private investors.

The bankruptcy judge ruled in favor of the company. In 2002, Polaroid was sold to One Equity Partners, an investment firm with a special interest in financially distressed businesses. (One Equity was a unit of Bank One Corp., now part of JPMorgan Chase.) Many retirees believed the purchase price of $255 million was only a fraction of the old Polaroid's value. There was evidence supporting that view: The new owners financed their purchase, in part, with $138 million of Polaroid's own cash.

Employees did not leave bankruptcy court empty-handed. They all got something in the mail. Moss will never forget the day hers arrived.

"I got a check for $47," she recalled. She had lost tens of thousands of dollars in ESOP contributions, health benefits, and severance payments. Now she and the rest of Polaroid's other six thousand retirees were being compensated with $47 checks. "You should have heard the jokes," she said. "How about we all meet at McDonald's and spend our $47 checks?"

Under a new management team headed by Jacques Nasser, former chairman of the Ford Motor Company, Polaroid returned to profitability almost overnight. Little more than two years after the company emerged from bankruptcy, One Equity sold it to a Minnesota entrepreneur for $426,000,000 in cash. The new managers, who had received stock in the post-bankruptcy Polaroid, walked away with millions of dollars. Nasser got $12.8 million for his one million shares.

Other executives and directors were rewarded for their efforts. Rick Lazio, four-term Republican from West Islip, New York, who effectively gave up his House seat for an unsuccessful Senate run against Hillary Rodham Clinton in 2000, collected $512,675 for a brief stint as a director. That amounted to nearly twice the $282,000 paid to all six thousand retirees. The $12.08 a share that the new managers received for little more than two years work was 134 times the 9¢ a share handed out earlier to lifelong workers.

Chapter 5

Let's Break a Deal

Washington has a rich history of catering to special and corporate interests at the expense of ordinary citizens. Nowhere is this more evident than in legislation dealing with company pensions.

It has been this way since 1964, when carmaker Studebaker Corp. collapsed after sixty years, junking the promised pensions of four thousand workers not yet eligible for retirement, pensions the company had spelled out in brochures for years:

"You may be a long way from retirement age now. Still, it's good to know that Studebaker is building up a fund for you, so that when you reach retirement age, you can settle down on a farm, visit around the country, or just take it easy and know that you'll still be getting a regular monthly pension paid for entirely by the company." [15]

Oops. There Oughta Be a Law.

It took Congress ten years to respond to the Studebaker pension abandonment by writing the Employee Retirement Income Security Act (ERISA) of 1974. It established minimum standards for retirement plans in private industry and created the PBGC (Pension Benefit Guaranty Corp.) to guarantee them. Then-President Gerald Ford summed up the measure when he signed it into law that Labor Day:

"This legislation will alleviate the fears and the anxiety of people who are on the production lines or in the mines or elsewhere, in that they now know that their investment in private pension funds will be better protected." [16]

Another group that had no pension worries would turn out to be the biggest winners under the bill. Congress wrote the law so broadly that moneymen could dip into pension funds and remove cash set aside for workers' retirement. During the 1980s, that's exactly what a cast of corporate raiders, speculators, Wall Street buyout firms, and company executives did with a vengeance. Throughout the decade, they walked away with an estimated $21 billion earmarked for workers' retirement pay.

The raiders insisted that they took only excess assets that weren't needed. Among the pension buccaneers: Meshulam Riklis, a once-flamboyant, Beverly Hills, California, takeover artist who skimmed millions from several companies, including the McCrory Corp., the onetime retail fixture of Middle America that is now gone; and the late Victor Posner, the Miami Beach corporate raider who siphoned millions of dollars from more than half a dozen different companies, including Fischbach Corp., a New York electrical contractor that he drove to the edge of extinction. Those two raiders alone raked off about $100 million in workers' retirement dollars—all perfectly legal, thanks to Congress.

By the time all the billions of dollars were gone, and the public outcry had grown too loud to ignore, Congress in 1990 belatedly rewrote the rules and imposed an excise tax on money removed from pension funds. The raids slowed to a trickle.

During those same years, the PBGC, which insures private pension plans, published an annual list of the fifty most underfunded of those plans. In shining a spotlight on those that had fallen behind in their contributions, the agency hoped to prod companies to keep current.

Corporations hated the list. They maintained that the PBGC's methodology did not reflect the true financial condition of their pension plans. After all, as long as the stock market went up—and never down or sideways—the pension plans would be adequately funded.

Congress liked that reasoning, and in 1994, reacting to corporate claims that the underfunded list caused needless anxiety among employees, voted to keep the data secret. When the PBGC killed its Top 50 list, David M. Strauss, then the agency's executive director, explained, "With full implementation of [the 1994 pension law], we now have better tools in place." [17]

PBGC officials were so bullish about those "better tools," including provisions to levy higher fees on companies ignoring obligations to their employees; they predicted that underfunded pension plans would be a thing of the past. As a story in *The Los Angeles Times* put it, "PBGC officials said the act nearly guarantees that large, underfunded plans will strengthen and the chronic deficits suffered by the pension guaranty organization will be eliminated within ten years" [18]

Not even close; instead, pension plan deficits accelerated at warp speed. In 1994, the deficit in PBGC plans was $31 billion. The Pension Benefit Guaranty Corporation today released its Fiscal Year 2016 Annual Report showing the deficit in its multiemployer insurance program rose to $58.8 billion. The increase was driven by additional multiemployer plans that are expected to run out of money within the next 10 years, and by decreases in interest factors used to value PBGC's liabilities.

Since the PBGC no longer publishes its Top 50 list, anyone looking for even remotely comparable information about underfunded pension plans must sift through the voluminous filings of individual companies with the SEC or the Labor Department, where pension plan finances are recorded, or turn to the reports of independent firms such as Standard & Poors. The findings aren't reassuring.

According to S&P Sara Lee Corp. of Chicago, a global maker of food products ended 2004 with a pension deficit of $1.5 billion. The company's pension plans held enough assets to cover 69.8 percent of promised retirement pay. Ford Motor Company's deficit came in at $12.3 billion. Ford could write retirement checks for 83 percent of money owed. ExxonMobil Corp. was down $11.5 billion, with enough money to issue retirement checks covering 61 percent of promised benefits. Exxon had extracted $1.6 billion from its pension plans in 1986 because they were deemed overfunded. The company explained then that "our shareholders would be better served" that way."

In reality, the deficits in many cases are worse than the published data suggest, which becomes evident when bankrupt corporations dump their pension plans on the PBGC. Time after time, the agency has discovered, the gap between retirement holdings and pensions owed was much wider than the companies had reported to stockholders or employees.

Thus, LTV Corp., the giant Cleveland steelmaker, reported that its plan for hourly workers was about 80 percent funded, but when it was turned over to the PBGC, there were assets to cover only 52 percent of benefits—a shortfall of $1.6 billion to be assumed by the agency.

How can this be? Thanks to the way Congress writes the rules, pension accounting has a lot in common with Enron accounting, but with one exception: It's perfectly legal. By adjusting the arcane formulas used to calculate pension assets and obligations, corporate accountants can turn a drastically underfunded system into a financially healthy one, even inflate a company's profits and push up its stock price. Ethan Kra, chief actuary of Mercer Human Resources Consulting, once put it this way: "If you used the same accounting for the operations side [of a corporation] that is used on pension funds, you would be put in jail." [19]

The old PBGC lists of deadbeat pension funds served another purpose. They were an early warning sign of companies in trouble—a sign often ignored or denied by the companies themselves. "Somehow, if companies are making progress toward an objective that's consistent with [the PBGC's], then I think it's counterproductive to be exposed on this public listing," complained Gary Millenbruch, executive vice president of Bethlehem Steel, a perennial favorite on the Top 50. [20]

Time proved Millenbruch wrong. The early warnings about Bethlehem's pension liabilities turned out to be right on target. Bethlehem Steel eventually filed for bankruptcy, and the PBGC took over its pension plans, which were short $3.7 billion. The company, once America's second-largest steelmaker, no longer exists. In the Top 50 pension deadbeats of 1990 the PBGC reported that the funds of Pan Am Corp., operator of what was once the premier global airline, had only one-third of the assets needed to pay its promised pensions. Pan Am does not exist today, either.

Contrary to the assertions of company executives, PBGC officials, and members of Congress, one company after another on the 1990 Top 50 disappeared. To be sure, many are still around, like General Motors. That year (1990), the PBGC reported a $1.9 billion deficit in GM's pension plans. In 2005 by GM's reckoning, the deficit is $10 billion. The PBGC estimates it at $31 billion. As of FYE 2015, the pension plan is underfunded by a whopping $21 billion. [21]

As for the pension fund deficit, if GM or any other company can't come up with the money, the PBGC will cover retirement checks up to a fixed amount—$45,600 in 2006 or until the agency runs out of money. That's projected to occur around 2013. At that point, Congress will be forced to cover a cost of $100 billion or more.

When judgment day comes, other economic forces will influence the decision. On July 22, 2009 The Pension Benefit Guaranty Corporation today announced it will assume responsibility for the pension plans of 70,000 workers and retirees of Delphi Corp., the nation's largest producer of automotive parts. [22]

Medicare, which is in far worse shape than Social Security, already is in the red on a cash basis. In what promises to play out as a mean-spirited competition in 2017, Congress has laid the groundwork to pit individual citizens against one another to fight over the budget scraps available for those and all other programs. This was how the Congress under the status-quo saw this issue. 2017 brings a new administration that does not look at things from a political standpoint but rather from a business standpoint. In my humble opinion; this will make all the difference as our nation is rebuilding its stature after the last eight+ years of political hacks running this economy into the ground.

Chapter 6

Who's Left Holding the Bag?

In the meantime, pension plans that companies are dumping are so short of assets that the PBGC's financial position is rapidly deteriorating. In 2000, the agency operated with a $10 billion surplus. By 2004, the surplus had turned into a $23 billion deficit. By the end of 2005 the shortfall may top $30 billion.

As the Government Accountability Office put it earlier; in 2005 "PBGC's accumulated deficit is too big. The plans simply do not have enough money in the system to back up the long-term promises many employers have made to their workers. [23] To add to its woes, the agency has a record 350 active bankruptcy cases, according to Bradley D. Belt, executive director. Of those, Belt told Congress, "Thirty-seven have underfunding claims of $100 million or more, including six in excess of $500 million." [24]

In 2005 Congress idly watched United Airlines and US Airways unload their pension obligations on the PBGC. Delta and Northwest were positioned to do the same. That increases the likelihood that other old-line carriers like American and Continental will be forced to do likewise. Fortunately, this did not happen due to the Pension Protection Act of 2006. The pension act will give both carriers 17 years to fully fund their plans, vs. seven years for most other companies. Delta and Northwest have frozen their pension benefits so the debt can't continue to grow.

Northwest's CEO, Douglas Steenland, bluntly told the Senate Finance Committee in June 2004 "Northwest has concluded that defined-benefit plans simply do not work for an industry that is as competitive and vulnerable from forces ranging from terrorism to international oil prices that are largely beyond its control, as is the airline industry." In that, he merely echoed Robert Crandall, former chief of American Airlines, who told another Senate committee in October 2004: "All the [older] legacy carriers must get rid of their defined-benefit pension plans." [25] In all, the pension funds of those airlines are short $22 billion.

The sudden shift from annual pensions of a guaranteed amount for a lifetime to a lesser and uncertain amount for a limited period is taking its toll on workers. Robin Gilinger, forty-two, a united flight attendant for fourteen years, sees a frightening financial picture. She has another fourteen years to go before she can take early retirement. Under the old pension plan, she would have received a monthly check of $2,184. Because of givebacks, that's down to $776—a poverty-level annual income of $9,312 by 2005 standards even before inflation takes its toll over the coming years. And there is the distinct possibility it could be less than that. Her husband, who worked for 24 years, lost his pension in a corporate takeover.

Gilinger, who lived with her husband and nine-year-old daughter in Mount Laurel, New Jersey, at the time, was not planning on early retirement and certainly couldn't afford it in that situation but, she has concerns reminiscent of Joy Whitehouse's experience.

"It's scary. What if something happened to my husband or if I got disabled?" she asked. "Then I'm looking at nothing."

"Above all, what's frustrating is that we were told we were going to get our pension, and we're not. The senior flight attendants, the ones who've worked thirty years, they're worried how they're going to survive."

Each time the PBGC takes on another failed pension plan, it makes the pension insurance program more expensive for the remaining businesses. That, in turn, prompts other companies to unload their plans. The PBGC receives no tax money. Its revenue comes from investment income and premiums that corporations pay on their insured workers. As a result, soundly managed companies with solid retirement plans are compelled to pick up the costs for plans in mismanaged companies as well as those that just want to unload their employee benefits.

Critics feared a proposal by the Bush administration to overhaul the system would actually increase the likelihood that more companies would kill existing plans and that other companies considering the establishment of a defined-benefit plan would choose a less expensive option. Nothing changed under the Obama administration concerning retirement plans. An analysis of 471 FORTUNE 1000 companies by Watson Wyatt Worldwide, a global consulting firm, concluded in 2005, "Healthy companies would see their total PBGC premiums increase 240 percent under the proposal, more than double the 113 percent increase for financially troubled employers." [26]

Barring a reversal in government policies, the PBGC could require a multibillion-dollar taxpayer bailout. The last time that happened was during the 1980s and '90s, when another government insurer, the Federal Savings and Loan Insurance Corporation, was unable to keep up with a thrift industry spinning out of control. The Federal Government eventually spent $124 billion. Unlike the FSLIC, which was backed by the US government, the PBGC is not. That means an indifferent Congress could turn its back on the retirement crash. According to the agency's estimate, that would translate into a 90 percent reduction in pensions it currently pays.

Chapter 7

Where the 401(k) Falls Short

The universal replacement to the pension— by the consensus of the Bush administration, Congress, Wall Street, and corporate America—was the ubiquitous 401(k). As then President Bush explained at a gathering at Auburn University in Montgomery, Alabama, in 2004.

"When I was young, I didn't know anything about 401(k)s because I don't think they existed. Defined-benefit plans were the main source of retirement. Now they've got what they call defined-contribution plans. Workers are taking aside some of their own money and watching it grow through safe and secure investments." [27]

Tell that "safe and secure" part to the folks at Enron who lost $1 billion in their 401(k)s, or WorldCom employees, who also lost $1 billion, or Kmart employees, who lost at least $100 million. Welcome to the twenty-first-century version of Studebaker.

Truth to Tell, the 401(k) Was never Intended as a Retirement Plan

It evolved out of a tax break that Congress awarded to corporate executives in 1978, allowing them to defer part of their salaries and cut their tax bills. At the time, federal income tax rates were much higher for upper-income individuals—the top rate was 70 percent. (In 2016, it's half that.) It wasn't until several years later in 1981 that companies began to make 401(k)s available to most employees. Even then, the idea was to encourage saving and provide a tax shelter, not to substitute the plans for pensions. By 1985 assets in 401(k)s had risen to $91 billion as more companies adopted them. Still the amount was only about one-tenth of that in guaranteed pensions. As of Sep 30, 2015 The Investment Company Institute reports that Americans held $6.8 trillion in all employer-based defined contribution retirement plans in Q2 2015, of which $4.7 trillion was held in **401(k)** plans. [28]

All that changed as corporations discovered they could improve their bottom lines by shifting workers out of costly defined-benefit plans and into much cheaper (for companies) and more risky (for workers) uninsured 401(k)s. In effect, employees took a hefty pay cut and barely seemed to notice.

Lawmakers and supporters advocated the move by pointing to a changing economy in which employees switch jobs frequently. They maintained that because defined-benefit plans are based on length of service and an average of salaries over the last few years of work, they no longer met employees' needs. But Congress could have revised the rules and made defined-benefit plans portable over a working life, just like 401(k)s, and retained the guarantee of a fixed-retirement amount, just like corporations do for their executives.

As it is, 401(k) portability often *impedes* efforts to save for retirement. As job hoppers move from one employer to another, most succumb to the temptation to cash out their 401(k)s and spend the money, a practice hardly reflective of a serious retirement system.

In 2004, $2 trillion was invested in those accounts and in 2008; Stock market turmoil has wiped out roughly $2 trillion of Americans' retirement savings over the past 15 months 2006-2007, according to the Congressional Budget Office.[29] However, to understand why the 401(k) is no substitute for a defined-benefit pension, look beneath that big number. In 2004, the airwaves crackled with announcements that the value of the average 401(k) had climbed to $61,000; At Fidelity, the average 401(k) balance hit $91,300 by the end of 2014. While that's up just 2% from 2013, it's a jump of more than 30% from 2011's average balance of $69,100, Fidelity reported. Noticeably absent from these announcements was any reference to the median value, a more accurate indicator of the health of America's retirement system. That number was $17,909, meaning half held less, half more.

Nearly one in four accounts had a balance of less than $5,000. Last year (2015) the average 401(k) balance stood at $96,288, down from $102,682 in 2014, according to Vanguard. The median balance was $26,405 vs. $29,603 previously. [30]

So it is that in the end, all but the most affluent citizens will have two options: They can join Joy Whitehouse in the can collection business, or they can follow in the footsteps of Betty Dizik of Fort Lauderdale, Florida, who is into her sixth decade as a working American. She has no choice. Dizik did not lose her pension. Like most Americans, she never had one, or a 401(k). After her husband died in 1968, she held a series of jobs managing apartments and self-storage facilities, tasks that brought her into contact with the public. "I like working with people," she said. But none of the jobs had a pension.

Hence, the importance of her monthly Social Security checks, which comes to less than $1,000. The benefit barely covers her medications for heart problems and diabetes, which, she says, can cost her as much as $800 a month. The Medicare prescription-drug benefit, she estimates, will still leave her with substantial out-of-pocket expenses.

To pay rent, utilities, gas for her car, and other living expenses, Dizik has continued to work since she turned sixty-five. For ten years, she was with Broward County Meals on Wheels, which provides meals to seniors, some younger than she is. But three years ago (in 2002), when she turned seventy-five, driving 100 miles a day began exacting a toll.

To pay her bills, she got a job at a nearby office of H&R Block, the tax return service. "I do everything there," she was quoted as saying. "I am the receptionist and the cashier. I open the office, close the office. I'm the one who takes the money to the bank. I do taxes."

A widow, she lives alone in an apartment building for seniors. Her four children help with the rent, but she is reluctant to accept anything more. "All my children are great, but I do not like to ask them for anything," she said. "I'm waiting for myself to get old, when I will need their help." "For the time being," she was quoted as saying, "I'm going strong. I have to."

She doesn't have much hope that Washington will be able to help seniors like her:

"They don't understand what it's like to worry: Are you going to be able to make it every month, to pay the telephone bill, the electric bill? How much are you going to have left over for food and other expenses."

Her key to getting by each month is forcing herself to live within a strict budget. "You learn to live very carefully," she said. Although Dizik really would like to retire, she can't. "I will be working the rest of my life." Soon, she will have lots of company.

I put this article in its entirety in this book because the information that it contains needs to be known by every one! Even though this was printed in *Time Magazine* in 2005 and it is even more relevant in 2016 and millions of people probably never read it.

Part 3

Better to Have It and not Need It, than to Need It and not Have It.

Chapter 8

Did You Know?

The vast majority of people that I know seem to think that a 401(k) is like a bank account. On the surface, it may appear that way; however, the 401(k) is more risky than a bank account because the balance is tied to the stock market and therefore fluctuates. Another thing that people do not seem to realize is that in order to realize the cash value of their 401(k) accounts, they must sell their stock.

An additional stark reality is that the cost of living doubles every ten years. Many Americans ignore this fact because they think that there is nothing they can do about it. But they can. You can. Your "personal economy" is under your control, and the sooner you realize that, the better.

While all this information may seem bleak, there is hope. This is where we delve into the meat of what this book is all about. The first thing that most people need to do is to determine where they are right now; the second thing is to determine where it is they want to be; and the third is to develop a plan to get there.

The first thing we have to do is get things in order.

The steps involved in placing things in order are: grouping, analyzing, and prioritizing. All of the steps help, and while doing each of them; you go through all three every time you add more data. Recognizing the steps is not hard when one knows the process.

There are four important issues for retirees, pre-retirees, and those who ever hope to retire:

1. How to maintain affordable health coverage.

2. How to generate sufficient retirement income.

3. How to maintain your independence at advanced ages.

4. How to best leave assets to heirs.

Each of these areas will be visited in this book; however, these are not the only areas of importance. You will also need to find competent professionals to assist in developing a sound financial retirement plan.

Do You Know What You Should Ask *before* You Choose a Financial Advisor?

Since you are reading this book, I am going to tell you. You've probably already realized that you may need some help and good advice with your money, and let me tell you that knowing how to select a financial advisor can be more important than the decision to use one **because:** *Selecting the wrong financial advisor can mean the difference between financial security and financial ruin.*

You see, if a financial advisor is not really on the ball, or has more to gain than you do, or is looking out for his or her own best interests instead of yours...LOOK OUT!

I'd like to give you a couple of examples of real situations to see what I mean:

Example 1: Janet was a very frugal woman. When her daughter and son-in-law took a look at her financial situation, they felt really helpless.

They had thought about talking to the advisor who had "taken care" of her in the past but were skeptical that he could be of any help, especially since her current state of affairs was partially the result of his "help."

Janet had just turned eighty and was the picture of health. When I met with her and her kids, she was very positive and optimistic about life. I admired her strength.

She needed to be strong, because she was broke— real broke!

Her husband had died when she was sixty, and she kept working at the railroad until she was sixty-six. Finally, after all her hard work, and saving, she was able to retire.

The combination from Social Security and her pension of $890 per month of income was not great, but it was OK. She had received $50,000 from her husband Steve's life insurance policy.

It seemed like enough, especially with the house paid for. Until the repairs for the roof, the garage, the driveway, and so on ate up most of her nest egg. Not to mention the "bail outs" she lovingly offered to several of her kids.

And the increase in the cost of everything! Now, she faces life with $5,678 in the bank and an old insurance policy with a $2,000 cash value. She has monthly expenses of $500 to $700 per month which doesn't take into account doing anything like visiting relatives or buying birthday gifts for the grandchildren.

And all she wants to know is if anyone can help. I'll tell you, other than some budget help, there isn't much anyone can do. The financial plan she was running on with no map had led her into a dead end. Believe me; this kind of story can break your heart. It's apparent that she will be out of money soon and probably end up living with her kids. The thought of an independent woman like her who is forced to depend on the charity of her family is very sad.

Why Did this Happen?

With Janet's and her husband Steve's pension plans, Social Security, and the advice they received from their financial planner, they thought they had it made. Unfortunately, the advice they received was not based on a plan but rather on a product that could "solve their problems."

The only financial advice they had gotten was from a products salesman who called himself a financial planner. Instead of first diagnosing every situation in Janet's life that could come up and helping her with all the options to avoid making costly mistakes, this plan was just the opposite! There was no diagnosis, no options to weigh, and no strategic financial planning that could have saved her from such a pitiful state of affairs.

In place of good financial planning, she got product pitches and suckered into a lot of bad financial decisions that were good for lining the planner's pockets but certainly not hers. Have you ever known anyone who has gone through a similar problem, maybe a friend or family member? Can you see yourself in this situation either today or sometime in the future?

Please take note: **You are responsible for your financial future.** You must take the steps necessary to assure yourself of a financial future that is far better than the one just reviewed.

Example 2: Linda and Dennis had to figure out what to do with Dennis's distribution from his company's retirement plan he was getting in a month or so. They had been financially stable for many years but now had to deal with this sudden change in their life. Dennis used to be a sales manager at a national firm until he was victim to a rampant downsizing. Linda is an executive secretary. They were both fifty-four and lived in a nice home in the suburbs.

Now that Dennis was going to be without a job, they wanted to know two major things: First, what to do with the distribution; and second, were they on track with the retirement scenario they had been working on together for several years?

You see, when they first decided to get help with their planning, they had all the typical concerns that any American family has these days:

- Tax planning
- Education funding
- Cash flow
- Investment choices and diversification
- Company benefits
- Risk management
- Retirement planning
- Estate planning

Just like for all of us, these areas must be set up correctly to give a family the best chance possible to meet all their financial goals! Linda and Dennis had set up goals years ago, and by planning, they had always been right on top of the situation. Now, when this bombshell at work hit, they found out some interesting things, for example: Even with all the money they had already paid for college costs, they had enough set aside for their youngest daughter and would not have to use any of their lump sum distribution to fund the remaining school expenses.

Better yet, they didn't have to worry about Dennis's job loss because they can retire NOW; all the planning they had done paid off. If Dennis doesn't want to get another job, he won't have to. Linda can quit whenever she chooses. Is that great or what? As a matter of fact, Dennis always wanted to own a little fishing shop, his passion, and now he was finally going to do it. Good for him. It's amazing to some of their friends and relatives that the two of them are so well set financially because they were always just regular people. They were not millionaires or anything, just hardworking folks.

How did they do it? Is the constant question from their acquaintances. We know the answer, and it had nothing to do with luck or hitting the jackpot; it had everything to do with planning and getting the right help. You see, the right financial advisor is trying to coordinate and tie all these areas together; to work hard with families like Linda and Dennis to assure they are always on target to reach their goals. As you can see, there is a lot of stuff to know. The average person cannot keep up with the tax law changes and investment opportunities alone. As with most complicated things in life like medicine or law, you need help!

Making financial decisions without good information can be a big mistake. Once you realize that it can't be done alone, how do you obtain the services of a trained professional to assist you? Is there a way to separate the objective financial advisors from the product pushers?

Absolutely! Keep reading.

Chapter 9

14 Secrets to Choosing a Financial Adviser

Let's take a look at the fourteen secrets to choosing a financial adviser. Please note: Not all of these secrets are going to fit you. Pick and choose the ones that fit your situation. My comments are not intended to criticize any particular type of plan. I have counseled over two thousand people from every sort of background and orientation imaginable. No matter what I say here, understand that I'm trying to cover as many bases as possible. I want to stress that I am giving my opinion, and this information is for the general public. If you want to modify or add or subtract any of these secrets, feel free. For example, if you only end up with seven secrets, then you can call this the "7 Things You Must Ask" plan for choosing a financial adviser.

With that caveat, here are the fourteen secrets:

1. Ask for five references. Three references should be from clients, and two references should be from other professionals like an accountant or banker. There are three reasons for the professional references. First, any person in business should have at least three satisfied clients they can provide you with; therefore, client references alone may not be enough. Secondly, if a planner cannot produce two other professionals who will attest to his or her ability as a financial planner, he or she may not be respected by his or her peers. And last, other professionals in the community see all kinds of things and will usually be aware what kind of advice is available and what kind of quality is provided by different people.

2. Call the references you receive. Many people ask for references but never use them. Call all five people because you can never learn too much about the person you are considering using for your major financial decisions. Take a few minutes to talk to these people. It will be worth it.

3. Ask if they charge fees for their service. If they're not charging fees, they must be making money from the sale of products. If they are making 100 percent of their income from product sales, they must sell enough to make up for the people who did not buy them. If there is a price to be paid, it must be paid either by the planner or you. Who do you think it will be?

4. If they do not charge fees, ask them how you can be sure that the advice they will provide is in your best interest. Ask them to tell you how they analyze the situation and what process they go through to arrive at recommendations. What you want to hear is if they find out how you feel about your money and your finances. If they do, then, they will give you a detailed understanding of your income assets and debts, company benefits, and so on. Finally, they will work up an action plan that addresses all your concerns and gives you choices— choices of the different ways your concerns can be handled, with the pros and cons of each choice. Then, and only then, will you be able to choose for yourself which way to go. This process allows you the ability to make decisions from an educated basis instead of from salesmanship. There's nothing wrong with being sold financial products as long as they fit your needs and not those of the salespeople!

5. And ask if they sell products as well as provide financial planning advice. If the answer is yes, that is, they sell products as well as provide advice; this should not

be taken as a negative response. However, you should recognize the potential conflict of interest that exists. Although I have known several financial planners and advisers who did not let the conflict of interest influence their recommendations, those planners were a small minority. Therefore, extra caution should be exercised if the planner also sells the products he or she recommends. You must ask a planner if he or she has any special incentives or reasons to sell you the things he or she is proposing. If the motivation is to get you what you need, that's fine! If you sense from the answer that there is some hidden reason, you need to move carefully.

6. If the planner sells products, ask if the products can be obtained if no plan is prepared. Buying financial products without a plan is like having surgery without an exam. Call me crazy, but I sure wouldn't want a doctor to operate on me until he knew what was wrong with me. A doctor who performs surgery without an exam is an idiot!

The same holds true for a financial planner who sells products without first doing an analysis of your financial situation. If you take away the planning process, you're left with nothing more than a products salesman. Do not let yourself be deceived! Now, a plan might be many things—a short one pager all the way up to a thick set of charts and graphs, and one is not necessarily better than the other. It just depends on how detailed your needs are. Even if the written plan is short, the interview process must not be.

Garbage in: garbage out!

The best planning scenario is not a result of the actual amount of writing but because of the depth of the interview. The planner must ask about all your issues, not just the ones he/she can make money on. For example, the planner should ask you about your taxes, education funding, home financing, company benefits, insurance, estate planning, retirement goals, investments, and so on. A good planner knows how to get to know you, your goals, and your fears. If you feel he or she truly understands your emotions as well as your finances, then you are with a real planner!

7. If the planner sells your products, tell the planner you would be more comfortable implementing the strategies with someone else. Note whether the planner starts to squirm at the thought of you buying elsewhere. If the planner tries to convince you that no one can implement his or her strategies as well as he or she can, tell the planner that you will consider that fact after the plan is completed. If the planner has faith in his or her own ability, the relationship will most likely continue. Otherwise, you have probably taken the first step toward being told that you are not a suitable client for his or her service.

8. If there is a fee, do not pay more than 50 percent of the fee in advance. Although a retainer is often requested, most professionals do not require 100 percent of their fee in advance. And you should pay the balance on completion of the plan. This assures you that the job will be finished to your satisfaction.

9. Ask about the planner's financial background. As a rule of thumb, if you have significant wealth, consider only planners that have been providing financial services for at least five to ten years or whatever time frame you choose. Although there may be some very good planners with less experience, why take the chance? I was once an inexperienced planner; when I was, I got my experience working with people who were also just starting out. Select an adviser who has more financial experience than you do.

10. Receive a 100 percent guarantee of unconditional satisfaction. If they are so sure they can help you, they should back up that promise with an ironclad guarantee. The benefits you receive must exceed the cost of the planning. You are the only person who can determine the amount of help that you have received. And the benefit received cannot be determined until the plan has been completed. There should be no question in your mind that you have received more benefit than cost. If not, then the fee should be adjusted. If the planner thinks he or she can provide sufficient benefit to you to justify the cost, the planner should be happy to put it in writing.

11. Ask them how they keep up on the constantly changing financial environment. Do they get research from their parent company? Do they attend workshops and go to classes? Are they studying for an advanced degree? Do they subscribe to financial publications other than general media? Do they read trade journals as opposed to Newsweek or the Wall Street Journal? Let me assure you this is an important question. There is no way on earth anyone can be excellent at planning unless they are excellent at acquiring up-to-date, accurate information.

12. Ask to see the financial strength of the companies they recommend; not just a simple rating, but some details about their assets and how their debt load is set up. Ask how the company invests their own money. Do they buy US government bonds, for example, or risky real estate? Remember that most of the companies and banks that went under in the years 2006-2016[31] were loaded up with huge debts and bad investments in junk bonds, real estate, and the like. While there is nothing wrong with some debt and some higher-risk investments, they must be reasonable! Just like your mom told you, too much of

a good thing is usually bad. And also like your mom told you, look before you leap.

13. Ask them how many clients they have and how many new ones they plan to take on. It is impossible for anyone to handle thousands of clients with a high level of personal service. Make sure you feel you'll be getting excellent service and advice and won't just be a number in a too busy planner's schedule. While it is true that every planner can handle a different client load, it depends on personality, staff, resources, outside professionals, and so on. Be sure to find out how they get things done and how fast they can respond to your needs. This leads to another question:

14. Which outside professionals do they bring in on cases, and when do they bring them in? No one person can know everything about money. It is impossible. Therefore, a good planner will have one or more outside professionals he or she works with, such as attorneys, accountants, pension experts, mortgage brokers, and so on. The planner who says that he or she handles everything with the help of other professionals is ideal.

Just make sure that the planner brings in outside advisers when the need arises. And believe me, it arises every day. Anybody who does not have a relationship with these other professionals is not going to be able to get you the best answers in a timely fashion. Someone who works with these outside specialists will always know when he or she is in over his or her head in an area and will get you the help and the answers you need. This is the mark of a smart planner.

We know that these are sometimes difficult questions to ask because you may feel you are going to be insulting the person. *Do not hesitate to ask these questions, even if it feels uncomfortable!*

We're talking about your money here. Being shy has no place in this process. If you feel too embarrassed to ask questions yourself, have a trusted friend or relative ask them for you. Whatever way you get this quizzing done, just be sure to get these questions asked and answered!

Chapter 10

Planning Is the Answer!

Why am I so insistent about planning? Because getting the right help is so important.

For example, did you know the Social Security Administration tells us that 94 percent of all Americans will not be able to retire on the same standard of living they had before they retired! What the government does not tell us is that the cost of living doubles every ten years.

Why is this the case? Possibly because most people spend more time planning their vacations and evenings out than they do planning their family finances! Vacations, for example, are planned very carefully. When will you leave? What do you need to do before you go? What will you bring with you? How will you get to the airport? What will you do when you get there? How will you get to the hotel and around town? Where will you eat? What will you eat? And so on.

Are you that detailed with your personal finances? Be honest now. Do you really take the time to plan your own future in such lavish detail?

It takes a lot of time and knowledge to analyze and plan your money! I understand! Raising a family can be as much of a full-time job as work itself! There is little time left to study tax laws and other financial information.

Therefore, the job of planning your finances is often delayed until a more convenient time. This is a time that rarely comes; most people wait until their options are very limited and time is short. This puts one in the "reactive" approach as opposed to the "proactive" approach. However, you must plan for your future today because the future will become the present whether you plan for it or not. Remember: People do not plan to fail, they just fail to plan!

What might be the outcomes if you don't plan?

- Wasting thousands of dollars in overpaid income taxes.
- Earning an after-tax rate of return that is lower than inflation.
- Limited choices of colleges because of lack of money at retirement.
- Losing as much as 50 percent of your estate to estate taxes.
- Not achieving your financial goals.

Proper planning is your best chance to beat the odds and join that 6 percent who are successful!

Take any one hundred people at the start of their working careers and ask them how many believe they will be financially independent. I would be surprised if even one person answered that he or she wouldn't be.

However, forty years later, according to the Social Security Administration, one will be wealthy, five will be financially secure, five will continue working, thirty-six will be dead, and fifty-four will be dependent upon their meager Social Security checks, relatives, friends, or even charity for a minimum standard of living. Planning is the major difference between the 6 percent who were successful and the 94 percent who failed to accomplish their objectives.

Don't get me wrong. I'm not saying that planning will make everything perfect. That would be a ridiculous statement to make. However, after more than fifteen years of experience, I can tell you that planning will significantly improve the possibility.

Planning is the one common ingredient in successful ventures! It would be difficult to find one thriving business that does as little planning as the average family! If you find one, it has been very lucky. Do you want to rely on luck for your future? If so, the lottery awaits you. If not, financial planning awaits you.

What I'm talking about here is setting goals; executing a plan to reach your objectives; and monitoring your progress, making any necessary adjustments on a timely basis. Simply being told to buy financial products is not planning. The traditional, random method of buying financial products from salespeople is basically history. A salesperson who does not take the time to help you create a plan before selling you products is not doing you any favors.

Imagine the following: You go to the doctor with a stomach-ache. The nurse takes you to a room and talks to you about your symptoms. The nurse then leaves and returns a short time later with a prescription for a drug signed by the doctor. You are amazed by two things! One, the doctor prescribed medication without even performing a diagnosis; and two, the doctor prescribed the same medication last week for your wife's sunburn! How could two totally unrelated health problems have the same cure?

Imagine your surprise when you find out that your nephew went to the same doctor for asthma and received the same medicine! If you didn't know better, you might think that this doctor was benefiting somehow from pushing this prescription. Could you ever contemplate a doctor doing this? If a doctor did, the doctor would be kicked out of the business so fast that his or her head would spin!

Many financial salespeople do this on a daily basis. No matter what the financial problem is, everyone gets the same products! Whether you know it or not, this may have happened to you. There needs to be planning first, solutions last.

The only way to be sure you receive a plan is to work with a professional who will provide you with a complete examination before recommending any solutions for your problems; an adviser who recognizes the need for a thorough analysis of your current financial situation.

Part 4
Solution Mode

Chapter 11

The Truth

As you might have guessed, this is the only way we, R. Hill Enterprises, Inc. work. Initially, we provide you with a free, no- obligation interview to find out what your concerns are and to determine if we can be of help. Hopefully, we can show you, as we have for many others, how to:

- Possibly save on income taxes.
- Maximize your company benefits.
- Build a retirement fund that will fit your needs.
- Have enough money to send your children to the best schools after-tax rate of return that has the opportunity to safely beat inflation.
- Make prudent decisions instead of pressured, impulsive moves.

This is a very superficial snapshot of the procedure that is used by R. Hill Enterprises, Inc. We realize that in order for there to be total financial integrity, there are many areas that need to be addressed. We will be going into each of these areas in great detail in the pages that follow. First there needs to be a little history lesson. While we covered this in chapter 2, it's a good idea to remind ourselves what was happening then.

Back in the late 1800s and early 1900s, most Americans were self-employed; most were farmers or held positions peripheral to the farming industry, and the majority of black Americans were sharecroppers. The Industrial Revolution had just moved into full swing. Manufacturing was gaining a full head of steam. The need for employees was great. The corporations of the time needed a way to lure workers away from the farms and their own small businesses into the factories. They devised an ingenious plan. In essence, the big corporations promised the workers that if they spent their entire lives working for the corporation, they would be taken care of in their old age.

The majority of the corporations were built in the North, hence the huge migration of black sharecroppers and poor white people to the cities of the North. The plan that the corporations used to lure these workers became known as a defined-benefit plan. This worked out really well because the retirement age was set at sixty-five, and few people lived to retire. During this time, the United States of America, with the advent of WW I and WW II emerged as the world's supreme manufacturer.

The population of the United States grew tremendously; everyone was taught in school how to get a job. The corporations got bigger and bigger; people started living longer and longer, and then the global economy began to emerge. I would venture to say that none of the big corporations could foresee the size and scope of the entitlements that they had put in place.

There once was a time when America was a producer; now America is a consumer, and the workforce is finding it hard to understand this shift. Corporations are failing to make good on their promises. Competition is fierce, and unionized workers fail to understand that corporations do not exist for them to have a job; they exist for profits.

There was a lot of turbulence in the United States of America. Women's rights, civil rights, and union rights were topics of the day. These subjects are for another book altogether, but they need to be mentioned here.

Fast forward to the new millennium; the world is experiencing tremendous growth. Most of the third-world countries are now competing in the global marketplace. They can do the same quality of work for less money. The large corporations are relocating or outsourcing the production that Americans used to do. This presents a dilemma for the American worker.

The American worker can no longer rely on the defined-benefit plan that their parents enjoyed, unless, of course, you work for the government. The Employee Retirement Income Security Act of 1974 (ERISA) is a federal law that sets minimum standards for retirement and health benefit plans in private industry. **ERISA does not require employers to establish a plan**. It only requires that those who establish plans must meet certain minimum standards.

In essence, what this law did was to make all employees responsible for their own retirement and relieve the employer of this duty. So the "defined-benefit" plan was converted to a "defined-contribution" plan. The problem was simply this: Employees were not informed of all the options that are available under the defined-contribution plan. Many people also are unaware of the fact that in a defined-contribution plan, the employer matches up to a certain percentage of what each employee places in the plan. So, if your employer offers a plan and you decide to contribute *nothing*, then that employer is obligated to *match you nothing*.

Financial Planning

This is where we delve into the different areas of financial planning. First and foremost, the idea of saving is the bedrock of financial stability. The act of practicing delayed gratification is an area the majority of Americans do not understand.

In order for there to be financial planning, there needs to be control. In today's "give it to me now" society, most Americans fall victim to easy payment plans. Saving is not on their minds. Nor do they think about retirement. Average Americans are living paycheck to paycheck, and if they don't wake up, they will not be able to retire.

Chapter 12

Wills and Trusts

In the following pages of this fourth part, we will be discussing four areas:

1. Wills and trusts

2. Safe alternatives to the stock market

3. Long-term care

4. Final expenses.

In this chapter, we will address the first area wills and trusts. First we will define what a will is.

Wills

A *will* is a formal and legally enforceable statement of how you wish to dispose of your property upon death. A valid will allows your last wishes to be protected by law. It can be changed at any time prior to death.

Why is a will important? Without a proper will, you are not able to control who inherits your property upon your death. If you were to die without a will, your property would be distributed according to the laws of your state. All adults should have a will in place.

Dying "intestate" is the legal term for dying without a will. Laws of Intestate Succession are the laws that govern the distribution of property in an estate where there is no valid will. These laws govern the beneficiaries, the administrator, and who the guardian of your children will be.

There are three types of property that need to be taken into consideration when implementing a financial strategy: "real property" such as real estate property and buildings, "tangible property such as cash and jewelry," and "intangible property such as life insurance."

When there is no will and there is no surviving spouse or heirs; estate property is said to *escheat* or pass to the state. The state supposedly tries to find heirs for ten years. If no heirs are found, then the estate reverts to the state permanently.

While there are many types of wills available, every individual should have a will. The elements of a valid will are as follows: The will must be in writing; it must be signed by the "testator" (the person who is making out the will) and the will must attest to two or three adult witnesses who will not benefit from the will.

There is a clause called the "self-proving" will. Although use of this clause is not a strict legal necessity, it is strongly recommended that you prepare and use this clause with all wills. This clause allows for your signature on your will to be proved without the necessity of having the two witnesses appear in court. This will save time, money, and trouble in having your will "admitted to probate" when necessary.

What is *probate*? *Probate court* is the entity that processes the estate of a deceased person. The *probate estate* is when all of a person's assets go through the probate process. Last will and estate planning is necessary to ensure that the property you leave behind goes to the people you want it to. Without careful planning, your heirs may experience some serious tax and property ownership issues.

A *durable power of attorney* avoids *guardianship* if you lose capacity; that is, a person appointed by you steps in to manage the finances of your estate. A *preneed guardianship* is established if you are deemed a danger to others or incompetent to manage your affairs and may be necessary to avoid third-party interference.

What is a "living will"? This type of will takes effect before you die and usually when you are incapacitated and may include a "right to die" clause or "death with dignity" clause.

Your family cannot override your living will.

Trusts

What is a trust?

Trusts are a very important topic to go into, and I think a little history is in order.

Trusts have been around since the Roman Empire, about 800 AD. The English knights used trusts to protect their lands when they went into battle. American trusts have been used since the 1700s, when they were used by the Colonists to help protect their property from English taxes and government.

A *living trust* is a legal agreement in which a person owning property, the *grantor*, hands over legal title to his or her property to a second person, the *trustee*, who manages it while the grantor is alive. As grantor, you did not give up the right to use or sell the property; it is simply put in another entity's name to avoid probate when you die.

The reason to create a living trust is to avoid the difficulties of probate. A living trust also enables you to transfer your property directly to the trust during your life without court involvement. After your death, the person you appoint to handle the trust may then simply transfer ownership to the beneficiaries you named in the trust. There are also other options.

The attributes of a living trust are that they are simple to set up, inexpensive to manage, and can eliminate costly estate probate charges, attorney fees, and delays of probate. In essence, a living trust ensures that your loved ones receive their inheritance when they need it most, and you have the final say as to what happens to all trust property.

With a living trust, there is no waiting for an inheritance no public record of the beneficiaries or what was inherited and a significant reduction of attorney fees at the time of death. A living trust can be canceled or amended at any time prior to the grantor's death or legal incapacity. Living trusts can be used alone or with a will, and you don't have to have a large estate to establish a living trust. Living trusts shorten the time that it takes for your funds to be distributed by months or years. A living trust is very difficult to contest or overturn, and the best part is it remains completely private.

A trust is very hard to challenge in court. In contrast, one of the worst risks associated with filing a will is that someone may legally challenge its validity in court.

In a nutshell, the benefits of establishing a trust are as follows:

- With a trust, your privacy is assured.
- You control your assets.
- A trust provides "conservatorship rights."
- Out-of-state property is protected.
- Trusts are legally recognized all over the world.
- Income taxes are unaffected by a living trust, and upon your death, your heirs will save on federal estate taxes.

This is by no means legal advice. Proper counseling needs to be sought when considering implementing a trust. The goal of any good financial strategy with respect to establishing a trust should be to take out of your name as much money and assets as possible, for keeping your estate from the IRS and other agencies so your beneficiaries will inherit the funds and assets instead. There are different types of trusts, and a good financial adviser will be connected with a good estate attorney.

We have just discussed the first of four areas that we will address in this part of the book. All the areas are important, and they work best when used together.

The next area that we will discuss is safe alternatives to the stock market in chapter 14. But before we discuss this investment option, we should discuss common investment mistakes that people often make.

Chapter 13

Common Financial Retirement Mistakes

Underestimating Your Life Expectancy

A generation ago, it was probably safe to assume that men would live to approximately age seventy and women to perhaps seventy-five. However, advances in medical science have pushed those ages up at least fifteen to twenty years. Realistic financial planning for seniors should probably assume that at least one spouse will live to age ninety or beyond.

Are you thinking that you'll be able to retire when you want? In financial planning for retirement, many workers plan on working well into their seventies unless illness, disability, or mere fatigue forces them to reconsider. If you plan on working past the normal retirement age, do not count on the extra money earned to pay for essential expenses. Sound financial planning for your senior years would have you save a sufficient nest egg by age sixty-five in case health reasons prohibit you from working any longer.

The sad reality is that the majority of Americans between fifty and seventy years of age have spent their lives and their money driving the consumer economy. In my practice, I have met with people who look good, have nice homes and nice cars, and are in debt up to their eyeballs.

Settling for Low Returns

Don't let your fear of risking principle leave you with a guarantee of running out of money prematurely. Sensible asset allocation will substantially lower the risks of investing, including the chance that your money will not grow enough to meet your needs. Consider this: If you insist on keeping money in three-month CDs and T-bills, as many seniors do, your earnings will be so low that you increase the likelihood of running out of money.

Many people settle for low returns because they only know how to work for money and don't know how to have their money work for them. This is where the rubber hits the road. Getting people to take responsibility for their own financial well-being in retirement requires the willingness on their part to learn what they don't know—how to achieve financial security.

Back to Basics

If your expenses are more than your income, your upkeep will be your downfall! There is a concept called "delayed gratification," and it basically means that you are willing to do what others won't do now, so that you can do what others can't do later. This concept needs to be reintroduced to society as a whole.

The habit of saving money is a good habit to learn; a better habit is learning how to make money work for you. While there are many financial vehicles available—and there are no good or bad vehicles; they just are—you must get the financial vehicle that will meet your financial expectations.

Chapter 14

Safe Alternatives to the Stock Market

There are a lot of areas to consider when you are preparing to retire, including but not limited to inflation, the amount of or lack of diversification in your portfolio, health, and increasing life expectancy. This is why there is a need for proper financial planning. We all need to make plans in order to have sufficient funds to retire.

There are a lot of questions that need to be answered when constructing a plan for retirement. The first question in everyone's mind should be: When can I retire? As stated earlier, this is where a line-by-line itemization and inventory of all assets and liabilities are in order. Then, with that information available, a plan can be formulated.

These are the questions that should guide your planning to have sufficient income at retirement:

- How much money will I need?
- Do I have sufficient savings for retirement?
- How much is enough?
- Where will it come from?
- Do I have enough money to have more years of retirement than I originally thought?

At this point, we will start talking about financial institutions. There has to be a shift in thinking from what doesn't make sense to what does make sense. Insurance companies are financial institutions just like banks except for the fact that they play by different set of rules. Insurance companies must follow *mandated reserve requirements.* This means, for example, that when a *fixed annuity* is purchased the insurance company, by law, must set aside dollar-for-dollar reserves to cover all anticipated payouts. Insurance companies cannot use your money to:

- Settle insurance claims
- Pay overhead
- Settle bad debts
- Pay for any other nonrelated annuity obligations

The insurance company can only use these reserves to settle withdrawals and redemptions of annuity owners.

What Is the Difference between "Qualified" and "Nonqualified Plans"?

The term *qualified,* when applied to annuities, refers to the tax status of the source of funds used for purchasing an annuity. These are premium dollars that have qualified for IRS exemption from income taxes. The entire payment received each month from qualified money is taxable since income taxes have not previously been paid on these funds.

Qualified plans are funded with pretax dollars and grow tax deferred; there are maximum contribution limits mandated by the IRS, and income taxes must be paid on the total income when withdrawn. For tax-qualified annuity plans, the IRS generally requires that all policyholders begin receiving payments from their policies the year they reach age 70 ½, or if later, the year they retire.

Qualified plans may come from a corporate-sponsored retirement fund, and participants can receive lump-sum distributions from retirement funds such as IRAs, SEPs, 403(B)s, 457 plans, or 401(k)s. You have limited control over these types of investments.

In *nonqualified plans,* the contributions are made with after-tax dollars. There are no tax deductions for contributions to these plans, but interest grows tax deferred. This is the ideal situation because interest is gained on the money that the investor might otherwise use to pay taxes. Nonqualified plans purchased by individuals may include savings accounts, certificates of deposit ("CDs"), money market accounts, or tax-savings accounts.

Annuity

The annuity concept is very simple: The interest earned on traditional savings plans is taxed annually; when income is withdrawn from the annuity, only the gains are taxable and will be spread out over a number of years. Because a retiree is usually in a lower income bracket, the taxes paid could be minimal.

The historical background of annuities is that they were used as a savings vehicle as an income-producing retirement plan for investors in the seventeenth century. They were used by investors in England quite extensively. Annuities are still used today as a major factor in retirement planning.

What is a tax-deferred annuity? A fixed annuity is a contractual arrangement between an insured person and an insurance company wherein a premium or premiums are paid in exchange for an interest-paying plan that will provide a stream of income payments when called upon by the owner. Tax-deferred growth is one of the chief reasons why tens of millions of people around the world are attracted to fixed annuities.

The "Rule of 72" is a simplified way to determine how long an investment will take to double, given a fixed annual rate of interest. By dividing 72 by the annual rate of return, investors can get a rough estimate of how many years it will take for the initial investment to duplicate itself. For example, the Rule of 72 states that $1.00 invested at 10% would take 7.2 years (72/10=7.2) to turn into $2.00. When dealing with low rates of return, the Rule of 72 is fairly accurate.

There are two types of annuities: variable and fixed. In a variable annuity, premiums paid into it are placed into one or more accounts. The separate accounts are made up of equity accounts usually in a mutual fund. These mutual funds carry the same risks as regular equity investments. With the variable annuity, there is no guarantee on the interest of the principle because variable annuities are tied to market values, which may fluctuate daily.

In addition, there are many other costs associated with variable annuities not found in fixed annuities. These assorted costs may include but are not limited to advertising costs, premium taxes, and sales expenses. With a variable annuity, it is possible that principle may be lost just as with any market-based investment.

Fixed annuities are a different animal altogether. Fixed annuities protect against living too long, which is an oxymoron. Fixed annuities are the only financial vehicle that can guarantee an income for life. No other financial vehicle provides tax advantages and absolute guarantees like a fixed annuity.

There are many advantages to fixed annuities. Fixed annuities pose no investment risk to the owner as in the case of variable annuities; they are free of market risk. Fixed annuities are a safe method for the investor to enjoy a higher rate of return. In addition, fixed annuities provide an income stream that the investor cannot outlive.

Another great attribute of a fixed- index annuity is that your income stream will stay the same every month, no matter what happens with the stock market or interest rates. Your monthly income checks will keep coming for your entire life, no matter how long you live. This feature of a fixed annuity is called a *life income option*.

Safety of principle is in my estimation one of the best attributes of a fixed-index annuity because most investments do not guarantee that the principle will never be less than the original investment. Unlike other financial products, fixed-index annuities GUARANTEE that your principle will never be exposed to market risk. Your policy values will never go down because of market fluctuations. Your policy will only go up as your guaranteed interest is credited each month, until you take your income payout.

Some other advantages of fixed annuities are they protect and build cash reserves. There are no commission charges when a fixed annuity is purchased. The guarantees of safety, fixed interest rates, and income for a long life give the purchaser peace of mind. Earnings accumulate tax deferred until the owner receives payments. The money is invested in a professionally managed portfolio. The annuitant can terminate the fixed annuity at any time he or she wants; however, taxes must be paid at that time on the earnings.

A fixed annuity can solve several problems:

Problem #1: How can I increase my income without decreasing the safety of my investment?

Solution: Don't put all your eggs in one basket, diversify your assets, and use an insurance company with high ratings preferably, A to AAA. Ratings of an insurance company are based on analyzing its financial results and evaluating the management objectives and strategy of the insurance company.

Problem #2: How can you make sure your money is available when you need it? How can you get some of your money out without paying penalties and charges?

These two questions are about *liquidity*. Most financial accounts charge fees for withdrawals before maturity on the entire account value. With a fixed annuity, you have the ability to withdraw money when needed without paying excessive penalties or losing up to six-months' interest. Fixed annuities have many guaranteed, flexible, withdrawal options. This means that you can take money out without paying any penalties or charges.

Problem #3: Another problem is federal income taxes. The federal government taxes interest earned on checking accounts, CDs, stock mutual funds (except special tax refunds), bond mutual funds, T-bills, and dividends of common stock. All of these financial vehicles are taxable by the federal government each year when interest is credited. Even if funds aren't withdrawn!

The solution to this tax problem is solved by a fixed annuity because fixed- indexed annuity interest income credited to your annuity is not currently taxable by the federal government each year. You will not pay taxes on your fixed annuity interest income until you take it out of your annuity, but this is usually at a lower income tax rate.

State income tax is a mirror image of the federal income tax situation. And the same solution applies.

Problem #4: How do you make sure your heirs will be protected in case of your premature death?

The problem: Probate administrative costs and fees usually averaged 8 percent to 10 percent of your assets. Assets are not available to heirs until the estate is approved by probate court. The average time assets remain tied up in probate court is one to two years. All records of the assets are available to the general public. The court, in absence of a will, transfers the assets to those family members as directed by law.

Once again, the solution to this situation is a fixed annuity. A fixed annuity that has a properly designated beneficiary other than your estate will bypass probate and ELIMINATE all probate administrative costs, fees, delays, and publicity. At death, more of your money will go to those family members who you choose.

Problem #5: Is it possible to guarantee your monthly income and your principle?

Let's say you find yourself in a situation where your interest income, after paying income taxes, is not enough to meet the increasing cost of living. You need to increase your monthly interest income without adding any investment risk. How can you do this?

The solution, again, is with the fixed-indexed annuity. It is possible to increase your after-tax income for either more monthly income right now or more monthly income starting at some later date you pick and that will last for your lifetime and beyond.

You see, with the fixed annuity, there is no market risk, your money is safe, and you can count on a 100 percent return of your principle plus an additional return on your money.

Problem #6: Another concern for retirees is what effect their investment choices will have on their Social Security benefits. Interest income earned and created in most investments like mutual funds, savings accounts, CDs, and bonds are reportable as income, which may increase your income tax on your Social Security benefits.

Interest income earned and credited on a fixed annuity is not subject to either federal or state income taxes until taken out; such interest is tax-sheltered income as authorized by the Internal Revenue. When you take money out of your fixed annuity—depending upon the income option you choose—up to 85 percent of your monthly income may not be subject to any income taxes. Fewer taxes will be paid, and you will receive more of your actual Social Security income benefits.

Problem #7: Another area of concern is the charges and fees associated with financial planning. Most financial investments in financial accounts charge administrative fees, sales fees, and investment fees as a percentage of total assets. To avoid paying these fees, most fixed annuities have no sales charges, no monthly administrative fees, no state premium taxes are passed on, and no investment fees.

In summation, there are some vital steps you should take before you get ready to retire, and the sooner you address them, the better. These steps are obtaining a full financial statement and also obtaining a comparison of financial assets that will help you decide where your assets will have maximum protection while giving you maximum income. To help you make these decisions, you will need a competent adviser, not just a products salesman.

Chapter 15

Maintain Your Independence—
Long-Term Care

Statistics indicate that over half of all senior citizens (people age sixty-five and over) will require long-term care. Research statistics are shown below in figure 1-1.

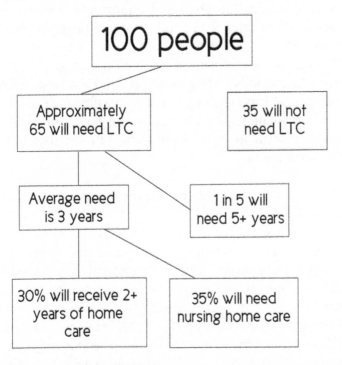

Figure 1-1. Percentage of senior citizens who will need long-term care sometime in their lives.

With such a great risk, doesn't everyone need long-term care insurance? After all, the cost of long-term care can run $6,400 or more monthly in some locations. So, if you have an extra $200,000 to $300,000 to pay for long-term care, you can self-in-sure and just pay out-of-pocket in case you are mentally or phys-ically incapacitated.

However, if you want to remain in your own home, get qual-ity in-home care, and do not have plenty of excess funds, then you want and need long-term care health insurance, which is the subject of this chapter

Long-Term Care

Have you ever heard the term, "spend down"? "Spend down" oc-curs when private or family finances are depleted so much that an individual becomes eligible for public sources of payment through Medicaid. This process of voluntary impoverishment is a transition from private to public sources of payment for long-term care. [32]

Here are some facts and issues: life expectancy is rising; the retiree population is getting larger; the ratio of men to women decreases in old age; you might find yourself taking care of a par-ent; seniors are more prone to disease and alcoholism; and a host of other concerns and fears. I will address these issues in the fol-lowing paragraphs.

Life Expectancy

In 1776, the average life expectancy was thirty-five years of age. In 2016 the life expectancy is eighty-four and rising. The re-tirement age of sixty-five years was originally established in the nineteenth century in Germany; of course, the average life ex-pectancy at that time was only thirty!

With the Social Security Act of 1935, President Franklin Del-ano Roosevelt set the minimum age for receiving full retirement benefits at age sixty-five. President Roosevelt died when he was only sixty-three years old; that was two years too early to receive his Social Security retirement benefits. In the 1900s, we had ap-proximately three million people age sixty-five and above. In 2016 we have approximately thirty-five million people age six-ty-five and over, with that number projected to double in the next ten years. [33]

The Ratio of Men to Women; Caring for a Parent; Disease and Alcoholism

In the population between the ages of forty and sixty-five, there are 20 percent more women than men. This statistic changes dramatically when we get to age eighty-five and beyond, with women outliving men three to one.

The average person will spend more time caring for an aging parent than his or her own children.

Only 20 percent of the people over age sixty-five in the United States are disease-free. Another area of great concern is the fact that the largest population of alcoholics is over sixty-five years of age. This is a very troubling statistic.

Other Concerns

Consider another question: What are the two biggest fears of people sixty-five years of age or older?

The first major concern of people age sixty-five or older is outliving their resources. To put that another way: How can they avoid running out of money?

The second major concern of people age sixty-five and older is Alzheimer's disease. According to the AARP, a full 50 percent of seniors over the age of eighty-five will develop Alzheimer's or another form of dementia.

This discussion bolsters the need to position oneself in a way that preempts the devastation of suffering from debilitating diseases. The best position is to have a long-term care policy in place. There are six "activities of daily living"—dressing, eating, transferring (from a bed to a chair, for example), continence, bathing, and toileting—that if a senior cannot perform on his or her own, a long-term policy is designed to provide help with.

A long-term policy also stipulates "levels of care," which are the following: skilled care 0.5 percent of people will need this level of care, which is seven days a week, twenty-four hours a day. The next level is intermediate care—4.5 percent of the population will need this care. And finally, there is custodial care; 95 percent of the population will need this type of care.

What are the odds that you'll find yourself in this position? In the United States in 2016 we have four million people in nursing homes; there is no telling how many seniors are in their own homes receiving some type of long-term care Out of the millions of seniors that we have in nursing homes in 2016, 90 percent end up destitute in two years. After age eighty, the risk of Alzheimer's is one out of two.

Consider the cost associated with long-term care. A fractured hip, on the low side, could cost $17,000 and the person with the injury would need to be cared for three to six months. If you're diagnosed with cancer, the average cost is $120,000, and the care could range anywhere from two to five years. The average cost for a person diagnosed with Alzheimer's is a whopping $323,000, and the care could last for as long or longer than eight years.

The next question you might be wondering about is: Who pays for long-term care?

Private institutions and Medicaid pay about 47 percent of the cost of long-term care. Medicare and other avenues (such as personal funds) account for less than 5 percent. Medicare provides skilled care only; requires a three-day, prior hospitalization; care must be at a certified Medicare facility; and they only offer semi-private rooms.

What does Medicare pay? Medicare pays for days 1-20, full benefits; days 21-100, only $128 per day*; for days 101 and more, nothing!

So how does one prepare for this type of situation?

There are a lot of solutions: Medicare, Health Maintenance Organizations (HMOs), personal assets, Medicaid Medical, your family, charity, and Medicare supplemental insurance. While these are all solutions to a greater or lesser degree, the real answer is long-term care insurance!

Let's look at some statistics: There is a 1in 1200 chance of being in a major house fire; the chance of being in a serious car accident is 1 in 240; the chance of having a serious disability is 1in 8; and the chance of needing long-term care is 1 in 2.

*Note: the $128 per day benefit is subject to change annually.

Will one or more of these events happen to you? No one knows for sure; however, your greatest financial exposure today and in the foreseeable future is not your hospital and doctor bills; it is the high cost of long-term nursing care!

Yes, long-term care insurance is something you should really consider. Your policy should include the following provisions:

- It should be renewable for life
- Require no prior hospitalization
- Provide all levels of care (skilled, intermediate, and custodial)
- Provide home health care
- Provide adult day care
- Provide hospice care
- Provide respite care

"Respite care" is the benefit that allows the primary caregiver a break from care-giving duties. It pays a daily benefit for care at home or in a facility, the care does not have to be overnight, there is no waiting period before it kicks in, and it covers fourteen to twenty-one days per year. I suggest that you choose the highest daily benefit for respite care, which is $50.00 to $500 per day. I also suggest that you get an "elimination period" (the deductible) of 0 days. You can choose the benefit term that will best fit your financial limits, anywhere from two years to a lifetime.

The available options on any long-term care policy that you are considering should contain the following provisions:

- Spouse discounts
- Premium waiver
- Inflation options
- Bed reservation
- Extended grace periods
- Restoration benefits

When should you consider buying long-term care insurance? Well, if you wait, your health could deteriorate and you could become uninsurable. If all insurance favors the young and healthy, then you should get it now because you are not getting any younger. The younger you are when you purchase a long-term care policy, the lower the premium.

This information is to be used as a guide only; your particular situation could involve some different variables. This is where you need a competent adviser to guide you in securing a long-term care policy that will meet your needs and fit your budget.

Chapter 16

Final Expenses

The following information involves final expenses. The act of paying for your funeral before the need arises is a gift from you to those you love. Funeral planning saves your family from stress; everything has been taken care of by funding your arrangements before the need arises and also saves your family from financial responsibility.

I really don't want to overcomplicate this last area; however, some consideration is needed. Why is it better to fund your funeral today while you are still alive? Prearrangement planning is a responsibility and eases the burden on your family of making decisions at a difficult time. With burial arrangements, it is not a question of if, but when and by whom. Some points to consider:

- Expenses double approximately every ten years.
- You could freeze the price and stop inflation.
- There may even be payment terms available.
- Will you be buried or cremated?
- What business will handle your cremation and burial?
- If buried, will you be embalmed?
- What is the nature of your final resting place?

Make your funeral arrangements known to your family. Don't put your funeral instructions into your will or a safe deposit box. A will or safe deposit box is often not read or cannot even be located for a few weeks after death.

You will need to consider prepayment of funeral arrangements very carefully. You could end up tying yourself to goods and services in such a way that make it difficult to retrieve your money if you change your mind. You'll need to read the contract very carefully before you sign it. Ensure that it includes answers to important questions such as the following:

- What protection do you have should the funeral home close?
- Under what circumstances are you entitled to a full or partial refund?
- What happens if you die while traveling in another state or another country?
- What happens if you move somewhere else?
- How much of what you have bought is transferable?
- How secure is the money you have put down?
- What are the state's regulations with respect to the fund in which it is held?
- What happens to the interest earned by the money in excess of any increases in the cost of the goods and services for which you have arranged?

The average family will spend over $10,000 for the cost of a funeral today (2016).[34] Life insurance, above and beyond any other final expenses you might incur, is a great way to ensure that your legacy is passed on without putting your heirs in a financial hardship, or at worst, forfeiting their inheritance to the government by virtue of not being able to pay taxes.

The first thing you should do when looking for life insurance is to have your expectations written down. The next thing you will need to do is be prepared to read line by line of the insurance policy to make sure your expectations will be met by the type of policy that is presented to you.

Keep in mind that there are no good or bad insurance policies; each is designed to meet a particular need or expectation. Most life insurance policies have everything you need to evaluate the policy in pages 3-9; be sure and read and understand these pages before you accept the policy.

Two terms that you need to be crystal clear on are *guarantees* and *projections*. In a nutshell: Guarantees will "happen" and projections are what "could happen." You need to have a crystal clear understanding of any financial products that you purchase.

I truly hope that you find the information in this book beneficial to you. As I stated earlier, the information is only meant to be a guide. In your search for a competent adviser, take into consideration what you have read here.

About the Author

Robb Hill is recognized as one of the nation's leading experts on safe investment alternatives. He is an independent financial adviser who has been helping consumers with tax advantage investment alternatives for the past fifteen years. He has created a service that caters to people who are frustrated with low-interest CDs and are rightfully scared of the crazy and risky stock market but still want higher interest on their investments and need a comprehensive evaluation of their available options.

Sound, Financial Retirement Planning presents a unique approach developed by Robb Hill that will solve all of your worries concerning financial planning.

R Hill Enterprises, Inc offers a free, unbiased honest, comprehensive evaluation of your current financial situation and informs you of any gaps in your financial planning within four business days of meeting with you. Guaranteed, a ($1,497 value)! You'll be able to rest assured, knowing exactly where you stand and the best route to maximizing your situation.

R Hill Enterprises, Inc. helps consumers find alternatives to becoming a victim of life's circumstances by preempting as many potential problems as possible! There are many strategies for each situation, and the professionals at R Hill Enterprises, Inc are experts at uncovering the best potential strategy for your situation. R Hill Enterprises, Inc. is based in Aurora, Illinois but services clients throughout the state.

Lecture Division

The best clients for this service are Affinity Groups, small businesses (10-50 employees), and churches.

Prominent organizations such a AARP, Manor Care Corporation, and the National Association of Retired Federal Employees have featured these lectures and workshops, and they have also been presented at many national credit unions and Fortune 500 companies.

The Lecture Series is offered nationwide and is customizable to fit your organization.

For more information visit:
www.rhillenterprisesinc.com
R Hill Enterprises, Inc.
PO Box 6464
Aurora, IL 60598

773.765.4491 office
866.393.1839 fax

robb@rhillenterprisesinc.com; www.rhillenterprisesinc.com,
https://www.facebook.com/rhillenterprisesinc,
https://twitter.com/robbhill2,
https://www.linkedin.com/in/robbhill2,
robbhill1@skype.com

Recommended Reading

Clason, George S. *The Richest Man in Babylon*

Johnson, Spencer. *Who Moved My Cheese?*

Kiyosaki, Robert. *The Cash Flow Quadrant.*

Kiyosaki, Robert. *Rich Dad, Poor Dad.*

Stanley, Thomas J. and William D. Danko, *Millionaire Next Door: The Surprising Secrets of America's Wealthy.*

References

1. Ehrenreich, J. H. (1985). *The Altruistic Imagination*. John H. Ehrenreich, The Altruistic Imagination (Place of publication: Cornell University Press, 1985), 48-49, 50: Cornell University Press. (1, 2)

2. Stanmeyer, W. A. (2002). *"How to Slay the Financial Dragon: Winning the Battle for Time and Money"*. J&W Business Group. (3)

3. Kiyosaki, R. (2001). Free Enterprise Celebration:Mind Your Own Business. Internet Services Corp. (4)

4. North, D. G. (2002). *"Reality Check" (August 1-8, 2002)*. (5,6)

5. Lechter, R. T. (2002). *Rich Dad's Prophecy (New York: Oct, 2002)*. New York: Warner Books, Inc. (7,8)

6. Steele, D. L. (2005). *"The Great Retirement Rip-Off", October 31, 2005 cover story*. Time Magazine. (9, 15-20, 23-27, 29)

7. *Fortune 500 continues to shed pension plans*. (n.d.). Retrieved 12 31, 2016, from Business Insurance: http://www.businessinsurance.com/article/20160222/NEWS03/160229986 (14)

8. Comerce, D. o. (n.d.). *wp-content/cps/CPS_March_Questionnaire_2013.pdf*. Retrieved 12 31, 2016, from U.S. Department of Commerce, U.S. Census Bureau, 2013 Annual Social and Economic Supplement Items Booklet – Feb/March/April 2013: http://ceprdata.org/ (10)

9. *401k plans reach 4.7 trillion in total assets*. (n.d.). Retrieved 12 31, 2016, from 401kspecialistmag: https://401kspecialistmag.com/401k-plans-reach-4-7-trillion-in-total-assets/ (21)

10. *Fading Fast: Fewer Seniors Have Retiree Health Insurance.* (n.d.). Retrieved 12 31, 2016, from Henry J Kaiser Foundation: http://kff.org/medicare/issue-brief/fading-fast-fewer-seniors-have-retiree-health-insurance/ (11, 12, 13)

11. *onlinelibrary.* (n.d.). Retrieved 12 31, 16, from wileyonlilnelibrary: http://onlinelibrary.wiley.com/wol1/doi/10.1111/j.1745-6606.1998.tb00401.x/abstract (28)

12. *retirement-savers-lost-2-trillion-in-the-stock-market.* (n.d.). Retrieved 12 31, 2016, from http://money.usnews.com (30)

13. *seekingalpha.com/article/3976982-general-motors-pension-problem.* (n.d.). Retrieved 12 31, 2016, from seekingalpha.com: http://seekingalpha.com/article/3976982-general-motors-pension-problem (22)

14. *www.pbgc.gov/news/press/releases/pr09-48.html.* (n.d.). Retrieved 12 31, 2016, from http://www.pbgc.gov/news/press/releases/pr09-48.html: (32, 33, 34)

CPSIA information can be obtained
at www.ICGtesting.com
Printed in the USA
LVOW03s1506220218
567559LV00001B/136/P